DISCOVER AMERICA

MONTANA

Krista McLuskey

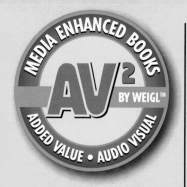

AV² provides enriched content that supplements and complements this book. Weigl's AV² books strive to create inspired learning and engage young minds in a total learning experience.

Your AV² Media Enhanced books come alive with...

Audio
Listen to sections of the book read aloud.

Key Words
Study vocabulary, and complete a matching word activity.

Video
Watch informative video clips.

Quizzes
Test your knowledge.

Embedded Weblinks
Gain additional information for research.

Slide Show
View images and captions, and prepare a presentation.

Try This!
Complete activities and hands-on experiments.

... and much, much more!

Go to **www.av2books.com**, and enter this book's unique code.

BOOK CODE

U 4 9 4 9 3 7

AV² by Weigl brings you media enhanced books that support active learning.

Published by AV² by Weigl
350 5th Avenue, 59th Floor
New York, NY 10118
Website: www.av2books.com

Library of Congress Cataloging-in-Publication Data
Names: McLuskey, Krista, 1974- author.
Title: Montana : the Treasure State / Krista McLuskey.
Description: New York, NY : AV2 by Weigl, [2016] | Series: Discover America | Includes index.
Identifiers: LCCN 2015048022 (print) | LCCN 2015048326 (ebook) | ISBN 9781489648938 (hard cover : alk. paper) | ISBN 9781489648945 (soft cover : alk. paper) | ISBN 9781489648952 (Multi-User eBook)
Subjects: LCSH: Montana--Juvenile literature.
Classification: LCC F731.3 .M383 2016 (print) | LCC F731.3 (ebook) | DDC 978.6--dc23
LC record available at http://lccn.loc.gov/2015048022

Printed in the United States of America, in Brainerd, Minnesota
1 2 3 4 5 6 7 8 9 20 19 18 17 16

042016
040816

Project Coordinator Heather Kissock
Art Director Terry Paulhus

Photo Credits
Every reasonable effort has been made to trace ownership and to obtain permission to reprint copyright material. The publisher would be pleased to have any errors or omissions brought to their attention so that they may be corrected in subsequent printings. The publisher acknowledges Getty Images, Corbis Images, iStock, and Alamy as its primary image suppliers for this title.

MONTANA

Contents

STATE ANIMAL
Grizzly Bear

MONTANA

STATE FLAG
Montana

STATE TREE
Ponderosa Pine

STATE BIRD
Western Meadowlark

STATE FLOWER
Bitterroot

STATE SEAL
Montana

Nickname
The Treasure State

Motto
Oro y plata
(Gold and Silver)

Song
"Montana," words by Charles Cohan
and music by Joseph E. Howard

Population
(2010 Census) 989,415
Ranked 44th state

Entered the Union
November 8, 1889, as the 41st state

Capital
Helena

Discover Montana

When Meriwether Lewis and William Clark first explored Montana in the early 1800s, they were awestruck by the open plains and delighted by the wide range of animals that roamed the land. After reaching the Great Falls, which is on the Missouri River in what is now Montana, Lewis wrote in his journal that it was "the grandest sight" that he had "ever beheld."

Today, much of the landscape that Lewis and Clark crossed remains unchanged. The dense forests, rugged mountains, and rushing rivers are still abundant with fish and other wildlife. The river canyons, mountain meadows, and Great Plains of Montana have earned the state the unofficial nickname of the "Last Best Place."

Montana is one of the few states left without big-city noise, pollution, and crowds. Skyscrapers are scarce, and the population is relatively small. In fact, there are fewer people in the entire state than there are in many U.S. cities. Many Montanans live on ranches or farms, away from the fast pace of **urban** life.

A number of Montanans depend on the land for their livelihood, including farmers, ranchers, miners, and loggers. Residents also cherish the land for what it offers in recreation. People who love the outdoors can hike, camp, fish, and ski in the natural beauty of the state. In fact, many people move to Montana to pursue outdoor activities, such as fly fishing, downhill skiing, and snowboarding. It is no coincidence that some members of the U.S. Snowboard Team live in Montana year round.

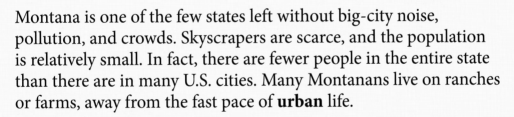

The Land

Montana's **name** is from the **Spanish word** meaning **"mountainous."**

Montana is the largest land-locked state in the **United States.**

More than 1.5 million people visit Glacier National Park every year.

Helena began as a mining town during the 1860s gold rush. More than 3,000 people flocked to the town during this time, creating a population boom.

Beginnings

Montana is located in the northwestern United States. In 1805, Lewis and Clark entered the area. For five months, they traveled up the Missouri and Jefferson Rivers, along Montana's Bitterroot Mountains, and experienced a land with more grizzly bears than people. While Lewis and Clark searched, in vain, for the **northwest passage**, they discovered the beautiful wilderness of Montana and the west along the way.

Native Americans were the first residents of the state. The Crows, Cheyenne, and Blackfeet were the three main Native American people in the area. The early 1800s brought the fur trade and the first small influx of European settlers.

It was not until gold was discovered in the 1860s that more people traveled to the region and Montana began to make a name for itself. Gold was discovered as early as 1852, but even then the population remained small. It was not until the 1860s, when John White and other prospectors discovered large gold deposits in southwest Montana, that the state finally got its boom.

Where is MONTANA?

F our other states border Montana. Idaho is to the west and south, and Wyoming is to the south. North Dakota and South Dakota are to the east. Three Canadian provinces lie to the north. They are British Columbia, Alberta, and Saskatchewan. Montana has two distinct land regions. The Great Plains are in the eastern part of the state, and the Rocky Mountains are in the western part.

United States Map

Montana

Alaska   Hawai'i

MAP LEGEND

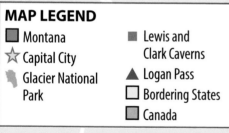

■ Montana
☆ Capital City
🏔 Glacier National Park

■ Lewis and Clark Caverns
▲ Logan Pass
☐ Bordering States
■ Canada

Helena ☆

IDAHO

1 Helena

Helena, a city of about 30,000 people, is Montana's state capital. Visitors can experience Helena's mining past by prospecting for their own gold just outside the city. Nature is right at Helena's doorstep with more than 75 miles of hiking trails accessible from downtown.

2 Lewis and Clark Caverns

The Lewis and Clark Caverns State Park is the first and oldest state park in Montana. It boasts one of the largest limestone caverns in the northwestern United States. Visitors to the park can take guided tours of the caverns to see the stalactites, stalagmites, and other mineral formations inside them.

CANADA

MONTANA

NORTH DAKOTA

SOUTH DAKOTA

WYOMING

N

SCALE

0   50 miles

3 Glacier National Park

Evidence of human activity in Glacier National Park goes as far back as 10,000 years. Drawn by the booming fur trade, Europeans arrived in the area in the early 1800s. Today, guests can enjoy more than 700 miles of hiking trails and experience historic **chalets** and lodges.

4 Logan Pass

Located inside Glacier National Park, Logan Pass sits between Reynolds Mountain and Clements Mountain. Wild flowers blanket the area in the spring and summer. The area is also a popular spot for viewing wildlife. Big horn sheep and mountain goats are common. Grizzly bears can also be seen on occasion.

Land Features

The Rocky Mountains cover the western third of the state. More than 50 mountain ranges make up Montana's Rockies. Glaciers and rivers are found in the mountainous areas, too. Some of these rivers flow westward, toward the Kootenai and Clark Fork Rivers. Others move eastward, to the Yellowstone and Missouri Rivers.

The land is constantly changing but stays beautiful. Melting glaciers slowly move rocks and debris. Forest fires, often sparked by lightning, destroy many acres annually, yet the fires are followed by new tree growth.

Missouri River

The Missouri River is one of the longest rivers in the United States. It begins where the Gallatin, Madison, and Jefferson Rivers meet in Montana. From there, it runs more than 2,300 miles, eventually flowing into the Mississippi River in Missouri.

Glacier National Park

Montana has 25 glaciers, which are ice masses that form in places where less snow and ice melts than accumulates. The glaciers move over time, usually a few inches per year, and most often downhill.

Blackfoot River

Melting snow feeds Montana's 9,686 rivers and streams. Blackfoot River and many other waterways are considered recreational destinations.

Emigrant Peak

Montana has 3,328 summits, including Emigrant Peak, which overlooks Paradise Valley in the southwest part of the state.

Climate

Montana straddles the Continental Divide, a geographical line running through the Rocky Mountains from which water flows either east or west in the continental United States. In Montana, the tall mountains create two distinct climate regions. To the west, the weather is mild. To the east, winters can be harsh. Average January temperatures range from 27° Fahrenheit in the west to 10°F in the east.

The state takes part in a network of National Heritage Programs. These programs track weather's effects on habitats and the species that are trying to survive. In Montana's wetlands, changes in weather and land use can greatly affect what happens to plants and wildlife.

Average Annual Precipitation Across Montana

The amount of rainfall that different cities and towns in Montana typically receive each year can vary widely from place to place. What aspects of the geography of Montana do you think contribute to this variation?

LEGEND

Average Annual Precipitation (in inches) 1961–1990

200 – 100.1

100 – 25.1

25 – 5 and less

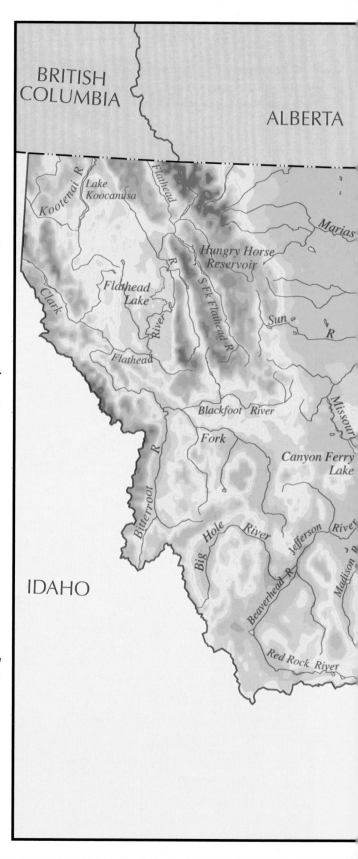

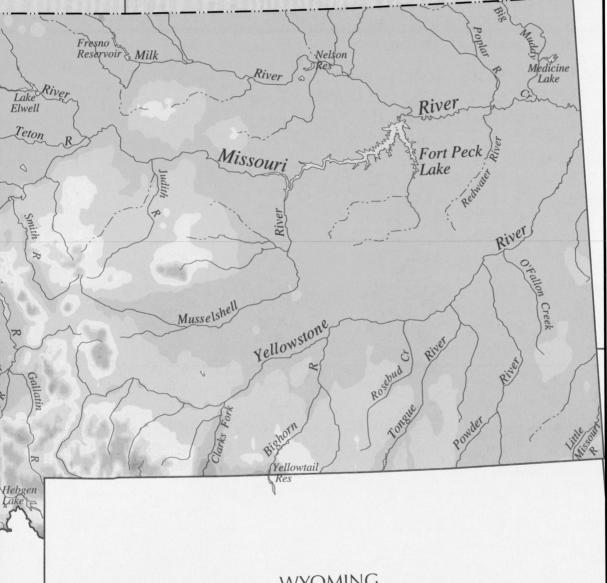

CANADA

SASKATCHEWAN

Fresno
Reservoir Milk

Nelson
Res

River

River

Lake
Elwell

River

Big

Poplar
R.

Muddy

Medicine
Lake

Cr.

Teton   R

Missouri

Fort Peck
Lake

Redwater   River

Smith

Judith

River

R

R.

River

Musselshell

O'Fallon Creek

Gallatin

Yellowstone

R

Rosebud Cr

River

River

R.

Clarks Fork

Bighorn

Tongue

Powder

River

Little
Missouri
R

Hebgen
Lake

Yellowtail
Res

WYOMING

Nature's Resources

One-fourth of Montana is covered in thick forests. Douglas fir, spruce, pine, and cedar are very important to the state's economy. Many of the trees logged for commercial use in Montana are from the western part of the state. In the northeast, in the valleys of the plains, and in other spots, the land is used for farming. Elsewhere, much of the land is used for raising livestock.

Coal, along with petroleum and natural gas, has been an important resource for Montana. Recently, production has begun to decline as reserves are used up. Today, the state's mighty rivers produce **hydroelectric** power. Nearly one-third of the electricity in the state is generated by water power.

Douglas fir makes up the largest share of Montana's lumber crop, at 32 percent.

Early settlers were delighted to strike gold in Montana. Since then, many other precious metals, such as copper and silver, have been discovered. In recent years, Montana's economy has relied more on the beauty of the land and tourism.

Located in the Bighorn Canyon National Recreation Area, Yellowtail Dam can generate up to 250 megawatts of power a day.

Montanans spend more than $4 billion on petroleum, natural gas, and coal each year.

Vegetation

The plants growing among Montana's peaks and valleys range from tall evergreen trees to grasses. The mountainous areas are covered with forests. At each level, from the mountaintops to the valleys, there are different, distinct collections of plant life.

The mountainsides are largely covered in towering spruce, pine, cedar, and Douglas fir trees. Wildflowers such as bluebells, asters, and brightly tinted Indian paintbrushes grow nearby. At the highest elevations, above the cone-producing trees on the mountains, there is a treeless area where alpine vegetation, such as dwarf willows, grows. Below the timber-covered mountainsides is the grassland of the valleys.

Cherry Trees

Among the plants most often farmed in Montana are cherry trees. The most popular varieties grown include Lambert, Lapin, and Royal Anne.

Douglas Fir

The most common type of tree found on Montana's mountains is the Douglas fir.

Ponderosa Pine

Native Americans often peeled the outer bark from ponderosa pines and ate the inner bark.

Nodding Onion

Early European settlers used the bulbs of nodding onion plants as flavoring in their cooking. Native Americans used the plant's juice to treat colds.

Wildlife

Although they are now rare, grizzly bears inhabit the dense forests of Montana's Rocky Mountains. Grizzlies grow as tall as 8 feet and can weigh more than 1,000 pounds, yet they can move as fast as a horse. There are six national grizzly recovery zones, and three are in Montana. They are Cabinet-Yaak, Northern Continental Divide, and Yellowstone. In these areas, grizzly bears are protected, so that their numbers can increase.

Another rare animal, the bald eagle, soars in the Montana skies. After being hunted to near **extinction**, bald eagles have begun to return to the region. Moose, mountain goats, and elk also roam Montana, in the west. The grassy eastern plains are home to herds of pronghorn antelope and deer.

Mountain Goat

The mountain goat can only be found in North America. Domestic goats look like mountain goats but are not closely related.

Ring-Necked Pheasant

The ring-necked pheasant and hundreds of other bird species inhabit Montana.

Cougar

Cougars, which are hard to spot in nature, are known as the Ghosts of the Rockies.

Grizzly Bear

The grizzly bear's blonde-tipped hair and its shoulder hump **distinguish** it from the black bear.

Economy

Waterton-Glacier International Peace Park

Waterton-Glacier International Peace Park has more than 700 miles of hiking trails.

Tourism

Montana's wide-open spaces, remote mountain pathways, and snow-covered slopes draw about 10 million tourists annually. Tourism employs tens of thousands of state residents. Yellowstone National Park, in the south, is a major tourist attraction. In addition, there are 43 state parks and numerous recreation areas and monuments to see and enjoy.

Rocky Mountains

Nearly one-third of the land in Montana is publicly owned and administered by the federal or state government. The vast tracts of undeveloped land include most of the Rocky Mountains, which attract tourists who ski, hike, and climb the peaks.

Yellowstone National Park

Yellowstone National Park is about 3,472 square miles. The park stretches into Wyoming, Montana, and Idaho.

Miles City

Miles City bears the nickname the Cowboy Capital of the World. The popular Miles City Bucking Horse Sale features rodeo events and live concerts.

Montana has about 18,000 dairy cows that produce more than 16,000 pounds of milk a year.

Primary Industries

Montana has nearly three times as many cows as people. The 2.6 million Montana cows provide milk and beef. There are also about 250,000 sheep in the state. In addition to milk and meat, the sheep provide wool, which is spun into items such as sweaters and blankets. Ostrich and **emu** farms have also been increasing in number.

Almost 30,000 farms and 57.5 million acres of cropland cover Montana. The state ranks among the top states in wheat production. Other crops grown in Montana include barley, sugar beets, sunflowers, and mint.

The **only** North American gem to be included in the **Crown Jewels** of England is the **Montana Yogo Sapphire.**

In **1888**, Helena, Montana, had the **most millionaires** per capita **than any other place in the world.**

Montana also has a large forestry industry. One of the state's great challenges has been finding a balance between logging, which employs many people, and protecting the land and its resources for future generations. More than two-thirds of the state's forests are open to logging.

The industries outside agriculture that employ the most residents involve trade, transportation, utilities, or government work. As natural resources become scarce, the major focus of Montana's economy has begun to shift. The number of jobs in tourism is also increasing, as are jobs in health and education.

Value of Goods and Services (in Millions of Dollars)

Many of Montana's industries relate directly to the natural resources of the state, including agriculture and mining. Increasingly, however, people are employed in jobs in the service sector, which range from serving tourists to providing health care or performing government functions. Why might this be so?

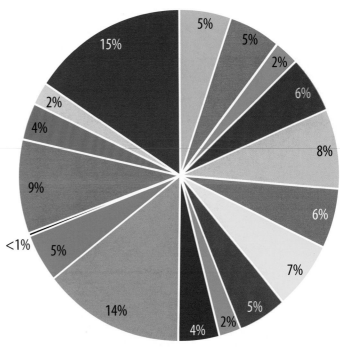

Agriculture, Fishing, Forestry	$9,048	Finance and Insurance	$7,091
Mining	$9,213	Real Estate	$24,046
Utilities	$4,044	Professional and Business Services	$7,738
Construction	$9,700	Education	$768
Manufacturing	$13,001	Health Care	$15,501
Wholesale Trade	$9,737	Hotels and Restaurants	$6,147
Retail Trade	$11,345	Other Services	$3,871
Transportation	$8,793	Government	$26,031
Media and Entertainment	$3,804		

Goods and Services

In stores across the state, many products display a "Made in Montana" sticker. The Made in Montana program's main goal is to help Montanans succeed in business. Products crafted or grown and prepared in the state bear this seal.

From jams to gems, Montana produces a variety of quality goods. The state is famous for its juicy chokecherries, plums, and huckleberries, most enjoyed in jams, preserves, jellies, and syrups. Yogo sapphires from western Montana are crafted into fine jewelry. Copper bracelets, belt buckles, and cookware are all made in Montana.

There is a high demand for skilled metal works labor in Montana. The metal fabrication industry is strong across the state.

Montana's workforce is known for a high level of education. Despite its relatively sparse population, Montana has numerous schools of higher education. Many colleges and universities are sponsored by the state, including the University of Montana and Montana State University. Several colleges have technical schools, which offer specialized training in engineering and other fields. Many companies find the skilled and educated workers to be a good reason for setting up businesses in the state.

The service sector has become the most important part of Montana's economy. It accounts for more than three-quarters of the state's economy. The many types of service employment include government jobs, jobs in finance, and hotel and restaurant positions.

Sapphires were discovered in Montana in the 1860s, and at least 1 million cut sapphires have entered the jewelry market since then.

The University of Montana is ranked number 48 in pharmacy graduate schools in the nation.

The horse was very important to the Blackfoot Native American group. More than just a tool, horses became a measure of wealth.

Native Americans

The Native Americans who inhabited Montana can be divided into two regional groups. There were those who lived on the Great Plains in eastern Montana and those who lived in or near the Rocky Mountains. The Kootenai lived in the mountains, though extreme winter cold would force them down to the foothills every year. The Crow, Cheyenne, and Blackfoot lived on the Great Plains. They became known as Plains Indians.

The thousands of bison, also called buffalo, that thundered across the plains of Montana were important to the early inhabitants. The Plains Indians depended on bison as a food source. Hides and bones were used for clothing, blankets, **moccasins**, tools, and tepees. To catch the swift-moving animals, hunters built corrals near cliffs and drove stampeding herds into them.

The arrival of horses forever changed the way Native Americans hunted. By 1750, most groups in the mountains and on the plains had horses. The hunters no longer had to wait for bison to enter the area. Instead, they could follow the bison on horseback and charge alongside their prey, hunting at close range.

Today, Montana is home to seven Native American reservations. Annual powwows and other cultural events occur throughout the state.

Exploring the Land

The United States paid about $15 million to France for the Louisiana Territory in 1803. This deal, known as the Louisiana Purchase, gave the United States a huge tract of land stretching from Louisiana in the south to Canada in the north. From east to west, the territory extended from the Mississippi River to the Rocky Mountains. The Louisiana Purchase doubled the size of the United States, and it made what is now Montana the property of the United States.

Timeline of Settlement

1807–1840 Fur trappers and traders arrive. So many beavers are trapped that the animal almost becomes extinct in Montana.

First Settlements

Traders and Travelers

1806 Upon their return to the East, Lewis and Clark talk about the natural wonders of the region that now includes Montana.

1805 A French trader named Toussaint Charbonneau and his Shoshone wife, Sacagawea, help Lewis and Clark find their way through Montana.

1841 Father Pierre Jean de Smet establishes a mission about 25 miles south of today's Missoula. He brings the Christian religion and new methods of agriculture to the Native Americans.

Early Exploration

President Thomas Jefferson sent Meriwether Lewis and William Clark to explore the new area, beginning in 1804. They traveled up the Missouri River, reaching what is now Montana in 1805. Upon their return in 1806, Lewis and Clark reported that many fur-bearing animals, such as beavers, lived in the area. This news inspired the next set of explorers to visit Montana.

Chief among the newcomers were fur traders and trappers, known as mountain men. Fort Raman became Montana's first fur-trading post less than a year after Lewis and Clark's **expedition**. Then, in 1841, a Jesuit missionary named Father Pierre Jean de Smet founded St. Mary's Mission, the first permanent Caucasian settlement in the region.

1866 Nelson Story reaches Montana with longhorn cattle driven up from Texas. This begins the ranching industry in the region.

1864 President Abraham Lincoln creates the Montana Territory, using the Bitterroot Mountains as a divide between Montana and Idaho.

1876 In the Battle of the Little Bighorn, Native American warriors overcome the U.S. 7th Cavalry, led by George Armstrong Custer.

1863 Montana becomes part of the newly created Idaho Territory.

1880 The first railroad tracks are built in Montana. Railroads soon increase the number of settlers.

1889 Montana becomes the 41st state.

Territory and Statehood

Miners who were unlucky in the California gold rush tried mining in Montana. Last Chance Gulch, now Helena, was the location of one of the early gold strikes in the area.

The First Settlers

Gold was discovered at Gold Creek in the 1850s, but the Montana gold rush began in earnest in 1862, when this precious metal was discovered along Grasshopper Creek. Hundreds of miners headed to Montana to make their fortunes. Many miners then turned to raising cattle on the open ranges as well.

As prospectors and settlers began moving to Montana in large numbers, the U.S. government moved Montana's Native Americans to reservations. Eventually, the Caucasian settlers were not content with that arrangement either. They also wanted the reservation land to farm and mine.

Chief Sitting Bull, of the Sioux people, was known for his fearlessness in battle.

Some Native American groups fought back in the Great Sioux War of 1876–1877, winning a historic battle near the Little Bighorn River in 1876. In that battle, Sioux and Cheyenne warriors, led by Sitting Bull, Crazy Horse, and other chiefs, fought and beat Lieutenant Colonel George Armstrong Custer and his soldiers. The hill on which much of the fighting took place, and on which Custer and more than 200 of his men were killed, became known as Last Stand Hill. However, by 1877, almost all of Montana's Native Americans had been defeated.

The Battle of the Little Bighorn is considered to be one of the worst disasters suffered by the U.S. Army in its history.

The Great Sioux War of 1876 occurred when the United States wanted to take control of the Black Hills, where gold had recently been discovered.

History Makers

The history of the state of Montana has been short, relative to the longer history of the United States. Yet Montana has been the birthplace or adopted home of many Americans who have made their mark on the national historical record. Many Montanans have made scientific advances, created important businesses, and served honorably in the military and in public life.

Burton K. Wheeler (1822–1975)

Burton K. Wheeler's first political election took him to the Montana House of Representatives in 1910, where he was a champion of labor. From 1913 to 1918, he served as the U.S. district attorney for the state. After an unsuccessful bid for governor, he became a U.S. senator, serving from 1923 to 1947. After public life, he returned to the practice of law.

Thomas J. Walsh (1859–1933)

Born on a train bound from Florida to Washington, Thomas J. Walsh was a lawyer elected to the U.S. Senate from Montana in 1912. During a 20-year Senate career, he dedicated himself to issues including child labor laws and gaining the right to vote for women. He is credited with exposing the Teapot Dome corruption scandal during the presidency of Warren G. Harding. In 1933, he was named U.S. attorney general, but he died before taking office.

Jeannette Rankin (1880–1973)

Jeannette Rankin was born near Missoula. In 1910, she became involved in the **suffrage** movement for women. In 1916, she was the first woman elected to the U.S. Congress, sent by Montana to the House of Representatives. She served another term in the House in the early 1940s. Rankin often spoke against war. In 1968, she led a protest march against the Vietnam War.

Mike Mansfield (1903–2001)

Democrat Mike Mansfield served in the U.S. Navy, the U.S. Army, and the Marine Corps. In 1942, he was elected to the U.S. House of Representatives. In 1952, he was elected to the U.S. Senate. He was the longest-serving majority leader in the history of the U.S. Senate. In 1977, he became the U.S. ambassador to Japan, and he served in that post until his retirement in 1988.

Brian Schweitzer (1955–)

Brian Schweitzer was raised on a cattle ranch in Montana. After serving in the U.S. Department of Agriculture, he ran for a U.S. Senate seat in 2000 but was defeated. In 2004, he was elected governor of Montana, and he easily won reelection in 2008.

Culture

With more than 28,000 farms across the state, the industry of agriculture is a way of life for many Montanans.

The median age of the residents of Billings, Montana, is 37.

The People Today

Although Montana is the fourth-largest state in terms of size, its population is relatively small. In 2013, the state ranked 44th in population. The three biggest cities by population are Billings, Missoula, and Great Falls.

The largest city in Montana is Billings, with approximately 110,000 inhabitants. Only Billings has more than 100,000 people. Missoula has more than 69,000 inhabitants, and Great Falls has about 59,000. The state's **metropolitan** areas are relatively few.

Western and southern Montana are the most populous parts of the state. About half of Montanans live in urban areas, and the other half live in rural areas. About 64 percent of Montana is used as agricultural land, such as ranching or farming.

Montana's population **increased** by **more than 80,000** people from **2000 to 2010**.

Q What are some of the reasons that people from other states and countries are choosing to move to Montana?

The Montana state capitol building started construction in 1896 and was finished in 1902.

State Government

Areas of what is now Montana have, in the past, been considered part of many different territories. The Dakotas, Idaho, Louisiana, Missouri, Nebraska, Oregon, and Washington all had claims on the land of Montana at one time. This was before the Montana Territory was established in 1864.

In 1889, the constitution of the new state of Montana was written. In 1972, the constitution was updated, and it governs the state to this day. The government of Montana, like that of other states, is modeled after the federal government. It has three branches. They are the executive, legislative, and judicial branches.

In the executive branch are the governor, the lieutenant governor, the secretary of state, and the attorney general. All of these officials serve four-year terms. Montana's legislature has 50 senators and 100 representatives. Senators serve four-year terms, and representatives serve two-year terms. The state's courts are headed by a Supreme Court with seven justices. Each justice is elected to an eight-year term.

The Centennial Bell, on the second floor of the capitol building, commemorates the 100-year anniversary of Montana's statehood. Every year, it is rung in honor of the Montana elementary History Teacher of the Year.

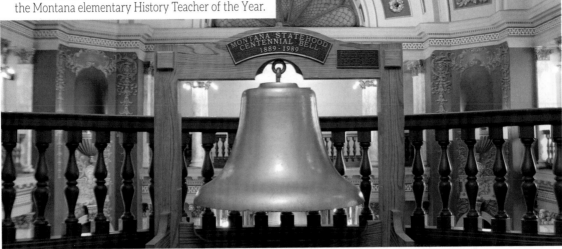

A statue of revolutionary politician Jeanette Rankin can be found on the second floor of the state capitol building.

Montana's state song is called **"Montana."**

Tell me of that Treasure State
Story always new,
Tell of its beauties grand
And its hearts so true. /

Mountains of sunset fire
The land I love the best
Let me grasp the hand of one
From out the golden West

Montana, Montana,
Glory of the West
Of all the states from coast to coast,
You're easily the best.

Montana, Montana,
Where skies are always blue
M-O-N-T-A-N-A,
Montana, I love you.
* excerpted

The Grand Victorian Ball is held in Virginia City, Montana, every August. Guests come in period costumes from the 1860s to celebrate the state's gold rush era.

Celebrating Culture

Many immigrants went to western Montana to work in the silver and copper mines in the 1800s. Soon after, more newcomers made their way to the eastern plains to claim the huge amount of land that was available for farming. At the time, Montana had too few people for the amount of work available, and Europe was facing the opposite problem. People traveled to the new state from Ireland, Germany, Poland, and Italy to earn a living and to begin a new life. Different ethnic groups settled in Montana and began their own communities. By 1910, one-fourth of Montana's residents were from countries other than the United States.

Wheat is Montana's leading cash crop, meaning it makes the most money. The state is third in the U.S. for wheat production.

Several religious groups **migrated** to Montana in order to practice their beliefs in peace. Mennonite settlers were among them, though many Mennonites left when the state government made speaking German illegal during World War II. There are also more than 45,000 members of the Morman church in the state. In addition, there are a number of Hutterite communities in Montana. Hutterites believe strongly in living simple, nonviolent lives.

There are three major Hutterite communities in central Montana.

Although they were once Montana's sole residents, Native Americans now make up only about 6 percent of Montana's population. Many live on reservations. Reservations uphold long-standing traditions. They also provide opportunities for education and training.

Powwows are held all over the state every year to honor and celebrate Native American history and culture in Montana.

The Running of the Sheep has been an annual event in Reed Point since 1989.

Arts and Entertainment

The calendar is filled with arts and entertainment events in Montana. In February, the Big Sky Documentary Film Festival in Missoula showcases nonfiction film. Living history weekends are held all summer at the Outdoor Living History Museum in Nevada City, which has one of the biggest collections of Western items outside of the Smithsonian. Bozeman holds the Sweet Pea Festival in August, a celebration of the arts that includes dance workshops and art exhibits and sales. In September, the Running of the Sheep through Main Street in Reed Point is part of a sheep-themed day that ends with a street dance, complete with live bands.

Home of the **Helena Symphony**, the Helena Civic Center is the **largest concert hall** in Montana.

Best known for her break-out role in *Dawson's Creek*, **Michelle Williams** was born in Kalispell, Montana.

Artists of all kinds have called Montana home. When Charlie Russell was 16 years old, his father sent him to Montana, and his dreams became reality. In 1887, Russell illustrated a terrible winter in Montana by drawing a starved, frozen cow surrounded by wolves. After taking an interest in Native Americans and their culture, Russell is considered to be one of the greatest painters and sculptors of the early West.

Montana-born Evel Knieval once earned the reputation as the greatest motorcycle daredevil in the world. In 1966, Knievel began his career as a stuntman. He performed dangerous motorcycle jumps, flying off ramps and sailing over objects. Knievel jumped over as many as 50 cars at one time.

The C.M. Russell Museum works to educate visitors about the art and life of the artist, as well as preserve is works.

Born in Butte, Montana, Evel Knievel broke 37 bones during his lifetime as a stuntman.

Montana is known for its world-renowned fly fishing in the state's many rivers and lakes.

Sports and Recreation

Fly fishing is a popular outdoor sport in Montana. The book and movie *A River Runs Through It* depict the rivers near Missoula as a fisher's paradise. In Montana, fishers of all levels of ability can be seen practicing their fly casting in open areas. During fishing season, people from all over the country head to Montana's rivers and streams.

As a Rocky Mountain state with snowy winters, Montana is also a haven for winter sports enthusiasts. Some of those sports are extreme, such as blade running. Professional skydivers jump out of a helicopter over a ski hill. A parachute keeps them in the air while they wind through a course of 10-foot-tall banners, called blades.

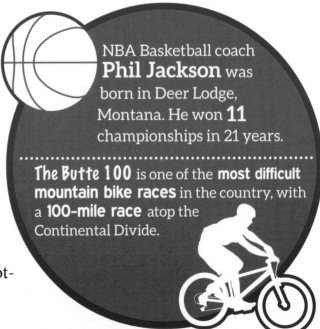

NBA Basketball coach **Phil Jackson** was born in Deer Lodge, Montana. He won **11** championships in 21 years.

The Butte 100 is one of the **most difficult mountain bike races** in the country, with a **100-mile race** atop the Continental Divide.

The state boasts many downhill ski areas. The lines for the ski lifts are rarely long, since Montana is a big state with a small population. Snowboarders are also welcome. Many of the state's ski resorts offer remarkable snowboard parks, featuring halfpipes, board jumps, and banked turns.

Montana is known for outdoor recreation, world-class ski conditions, and year-round activities.

For team sports, there are two main universities fielding teams that delight Montana fans. Signs of support are plastered throughout Missoula, home of the University of Montana Grizzlies. The scene is similar in Bozeman, hometown of the Montana State University Bobcats.

In 2015, the Montana Grizzlies were the Big Sky Conference Champions.

Get To Know MONTANA

More than **7 million** seedlings are planted **each year** in Montana to replenish trees cut for timber.

Montana leads the country in training **smokejumpers**, firefighters who parachute into remote areas.

Fort Keogh, Montana, is home to the largest **snowflake** ever seen, at **15 inches** in diameter.

From 1863 to 1865, more than **$30 million** worth of **gold** was found in Alder Gulch, where the Virginia City ghost town now stands.

About **10 million pounds of HONEY** are produced in the state each year.

The LARGEST **migratory elk** herd in the nation resides in Montana.

Montana has the second largest grizzly bear population in the U.S.

Brain Teasers

What have you learned about Montana after reading this book? Test your knowledge by answering these questions. All of the information can be found in the text you just read. The answers are provided below for easy reference.

1 What is Montana's official nickname?

2 What are the names of the two explorers who trekked through Montana?

3 Which city in Montana is the largest in population?

4 How many cows reside in the state of Montana?

5 The arrival of which animal changed the way Native Americans hunted in Montana?

6 What year were the first railroad tracks built in Montana?

7 The gold rush began in earnest in Montana in 1862 when gold was found in which body of water?

8 What is the most common type of tree found on Montana's mountains?

ANSWER KEY
1. The Treasure State 2. Lewis and Clark 3. Missoula 4. 2.6 million 5. The horse 6. 1880 7. Grasshopper Creek 8. Douglas fir

Key Words

chalets: wooden houses or cottages

distinguish: identify one kind from another

emu: a large, flightless bird, originating from Australia, that resembles the ostrich

expedition: a journey made for exploration

extinction: when a species no longer exists

hydroelectric: electricity generated by flowing water

metropolitan: referring to a large urban area, usually a city and surrounding suburbs

migrated: moved to a new place

moccasins: shoes made entirely of soft leather, first worn by Native Americans

northwest passage: a sea passage along the northern coast of North America, connecting the Atlantic Ocean to the Pacific Ocean

suffrage: the right to vote in elections

urban: in a city or town

Index

Log on to www.av2books.com

AV² by Weigl brings you media enhanced books that support active learning. Go to www.av2books.com, and enter the special code found on page 2 of this book. You will gain access to enriched and enhanced content that supplements and complements this book. Content includes video, audio, weblinks, quizzes, a slide show, and activities.

AV² Online Navigation

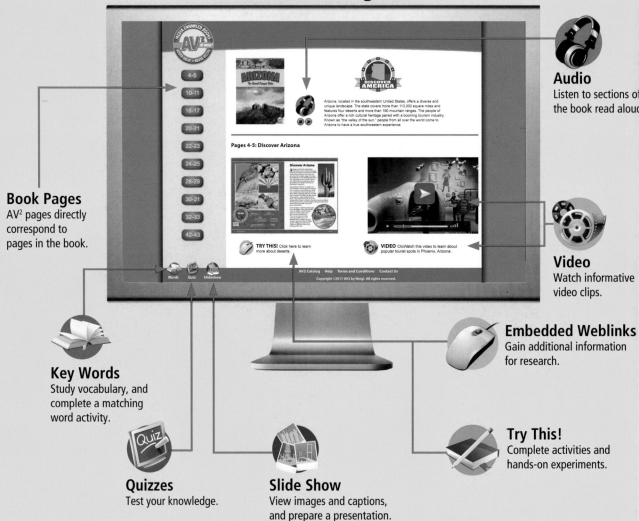

Audio
Listen to sections of the book read aloud

Book Pages
AV² pages directly correspond to pages in the book.

Video
Watch informative video clips.

Key Words
Study vocabulary, and complete a matching word activity.

Embedded Weblinks
Gain additional information for research.

Quizzes
Test your knowledge.

Slide Show
View images and captions, and prepare a presentation.

Try This!
Complete activities and hands-on experiments.

AV² was built to bridge the gap between print and digital. We encourage you to tell us what you like and what you want to see in the future.

Sign up to be an AV² Ambassador at www.av2books.com/ambassador.